The Hermitage Guide

To

The West Highland Way

Published by

Hermitage Publishing, Crieff

ISBN 1 898201 01 3

Nick Anderson has spent years stravaiging the hills and glens of Scotland, on foot and on mountain bike. Born and bred in Crieff in Perthshire, a location which is ideally placed for a life in the outdoors.

The West Highland Way

The West Highland Way is Scotland's first long distance footpath. It runs for 95 miles from Milngavie to Fort William. It was opened in 1980 and has proved a popular walk ever since. It is not a difficult route and well within the capabilities of the moderately fit, old and young.

I have designed this Guide to act as a planning tool to help you before you set out. It is not going to tell you what to see on the Way or even where to look for it.

What it will tell you is what the terrain is like under foot on each section, what to expect when you arrive at your chosen destination, whether you want 5 Star Luxury or a simple Bunkhouse, whether to carry all of your food, or what shops there are on the Way. It also contains contact numbers for the Tourist Information Centres en route; these are a good contact to arrange accommodation in B&B's although in the busy summer season I would advise you to book ahead.

When you decide to walk the Way, some of your friends may describe it as a dull tramp along boggy footpaths. To paraphrase Hamish Brown, there is no such thing as a dull walk, only dull people. The West Highland Way is a super walk, from the edge of the industrial heartland in the Lowlands, through the Highlands, to end on the West Coast at Fort William. You will cross all sorts of different terrain from arable farmland, hill farms and forestry, to bog and moorland. I would recommend that you walk from South to North to allow you to limber up on the easier Southern sections. Also, when it does rain, then you should have the wind and rain on your back.

The route of the West Highland Way is waymarked for all of it's length and it is relatively easy to follow. You will need to carry a map. The map of the Official Guide and the one produced by Footprint can both be recommended.

Build up your levels of fitness before you go and you will avoid spoiling your enjoyment of the walk. Before you set out spend a few weeks on some longer walks than you are used to doing. Spend your lunch hour walking instead of sitting eating. Use this opportunity to get your feet tuned to your boots. The Way does not need a great deal of fitness but if you don't have blisters or groaning muscles then you will enjoy it all the more. Take your time on the Way and don't try too hard on the first day. Plan your days with time to spare so that you can delay where you find things of interest and are not under any pressure to get to your night's final destination.

The bigger hills along the Way make for entertaining diversions and a change from walking on the flat. These hills are detailed in the text, but routes and directions are not given. They are serious mountain expeditions and if you are not capable of planning your route on these hills then you should not go up them till you can.

Mountain Bikes
The West Highland Way is a long distance *walking* route. It is not suitable for Mountain Bikes and **they should not be cycled** on the Way, despite what some Mountain Bike magazines tell you!

Dogs
Dogs are not allowed on some sections of the Way and it is requested that you do not take dogs on the Way.

What to Take

I decided to stay in hostels and bunkhouses which seem to me to offer the best combination of roughing it and the joys of home. How you plan to spend your nights will obviously affect what you wear and what you ultimately carry, and remember it's your back that's going to be carrying it all! It is quite possible to travel lightweight and to carry only a change of clothes for the evening with no camping kit or sleeping bag, though I would recommend at least one change of clothes during the trip. It would also make sense to carry several pairs of socks, since the one part of you that is in constant contact with the ground is your feet and it pays to look after them. If you stay every night in a hotel you will need to carry some clothes that are comparatively respectable to change into at night. If you are camping, then no one will be seeing you and you can be as scruffy as you like.

Walking
1 Pair Leather Boots. Depending on the weather they may spend 6 days immersed in mud and puddles so these are essential. It's no use spending £250 on a waterproof jacket and buying cheap boots. Comfort is the most important thing to look for in a pair of boots.
1 Pair Trainers, for a change in the evenings or a rest during the day.
Socks for above.
Walking Trousers; Ronhill Tracksters™ or Calange Stretchlites™.
Thermal Top, Vest.
Fleece/Woolly Jumper; a Fleece gives better warmth when wet.
Spare Fleece/Woolly Jumper.
Waterproof Trousers.
Waterproof Jacket.

In addition to the above you should be prepared for some rough weather and always carry the following with you :
Map & Compass.
Gloves & a Warm Woolly Hat.
First Aid Kit, and or a Blister Kit.
Whistle & Survival Bag.
In Scotland it is easy to experience all four seasons in one day, often in one hour, so you should always be prepared.

Evening
Whatever you feel comfortable in. It is best to carry a change for the evening whether in a hotel, B&B or camping. It is a chance to wash and change and have a rest from your day's activities. Have a look at some of the latest *trekking* trousers in your local outdoors shop. Some of these are very lightweight, windproof and reasonably smart. Look out for *Trial Size* bottles in your local chemist which contain enough shampoo and conditioner for one or two hair washes, but take up little space.

You will need a rucsac to carry it all in and the bigger the sac, the more you will pack in it. If you purchase a rucsac with no pockets then you can always add these as they are necessary. However, tidy people seem to like pockets to store everything away in its place. Again discuss your plans with your local outdoor store who should be able to give you the benefit of their experience.

Money. There are no banking facilities on your route, except at either end or at Tyndrum where the Clifton Coffee House/Green Welly Shop offer a *Retail Banking* facility @ £1 per £50 cashed.

Section II

The following pages contain the details of each town that you pass through and the details of the Way and the terrain to expect between each town and village.

Also listed are the hotels, bunkhouses, hostels and campsites with the telephone numbers of the local Tourist Information Centres to allow you to book accommodation. In the busy season it is always best to reserve accommodation for the night. It ties you to a schedule and although you may want to push ahead, it is better to be slowed down than to arrive at a small village and discover that there is no bed for you.

Hotels; these are graded by price for dinner, bed and breakfast but no assurance of quality is given.

A £ 25+
B £ 35+
C £ 45+

Hostels; the hostels of the Scottish Youth Hostel Association are graded according to facilities and size. These are very different from my memories as a schoolboy. They sleep roughly 6 to a dormitory and are spacious and modern. They have a lounge and cooking facilities. The Hostels can be booked but the booking will only be held till 6pm unless you have pre-paid. Allow around £7 per night in both these and the independent hostels.

B&B's; there are too many to mention individually. Contact the local Tourist Information Centre to book. Allow around £15 per person.

Campsites; phone numbers are listed.

Further Information:
Contact the Loch Lomond Park Authority Ranger Service who will be glad to answer any questions that you have.
Loch Lomond Park Authority Ranger Service
The Old Station
Balloch Road
Balloch
G83 8SS **Tel**: 0389-53311

Milngavie

Shops:
Butcher, baker, candlestick maker. Milngavie has them all. This is your first and last encounter with a town of any size before Kinlochleven. Stock up on any essentials from the chemist or supermarket.

Post Office

Banks:
Bank of Scotland, Royal Bank of Scotland, Clydesdale Bank, TSB.

Hotels:
The Black Bull Hotel, Milngavie, 041-956-2291 C

B&B's:
Various; contact the Tourist Information Glasgow to book, 041-204-4400

British Rail Enquiries:
British Rail Travel Centre, Glasgow, 041-204-2844

Route:

The West Highland Way starts from Milngavie Station and runs through the town to a large monolith which denotes the point where you step into the park and on to the beaten track. The going is good on a single track through the park and on into Mugdock Country Park. Waymarking is good and route finding relatively easy. Around Craigallian Loch you begin to feel that you have left the city and are properly entering the countryside. A short length of 100 metres on a B road takes you on to the next section through to Dumgoyne. The three kilometres or so on the route from Dumgoyne along the old railway track to Gartness are the most muddy and boggy of the whole West Highland Way. The mud is a cross between cement and super glue. Do not let this section put you off! From Gartness you follow a back road on a metalled surface until a you cross a field and into Drymen.

Drymen

Shops:
Butcher and small supermarket.

Banks:
Royal Bank of Scotland.

Post Office

Hotels:
Buchanan House Hotel. Drymen, 0360-60588 C
Drymen House Hotel, Drymen, 0360-60205 A
Salmon Leap Inn, Drymen, 0360-60357 B
The Winnoch, Drymen, 0360-60245 B

Hostels:
None.

B&B's:
Various; contact the Tourist Information Centre, Drymen to book, 0360-60068
Easter to Mid September; other times contact Drymen Library, 0360-60751

Route:

The Route from Drymen skirts the main road for about 100 metres before turning to cut through a field and entering Garardhban Forest. From here you are on forestry roads right through the trees until you are given the option of either Conic Hill (this section is closed during the lambing season for the last two weeks in April and the first two weeks in May) or the slightly less strenuous route through Milton of Buchanan and along the pavement at the side of the main road to Balmaha. The trail over Conic Hill follows a single track to Balmaha.

Balmaha

Shops:
Garage, tea-room.

Hotels:
None.

Hostels:
The Highland Way, 0360-87225/0360-87270
(Closed at time of writing but may re-open)

B & B's:
Various; contact Tourist Information in Drymen to book, 0360-60068

Campsites:
Camping Club of Great Britain and Northern Ireland, Balmaha
0360-87236

Route:

The track from Balmaha runs along the side of Loch Lomond until it reaches Rowardenan with a short section of only 200 metres or so beside the main road. The going is good along single track and is clearly defined in most places. The storms of January 1993 have done some damage along the lochside but there are no obstacles that cannot be easily overcome. The Way joins the main road for it's last 500 metres, before entering the trees at Rowardenan.

Rowardenan

Shops:
None.

Hotels:
Rowardenan Hotel, Rowardenan, 0360-87273 A

Hostels:
SYHA Rowardenan Youth Hostel, Rowardenan, 0360-87259

B & B's:
Various; contact Tourist Information, Drymen to book 0360-60068

Campsites:
Forestry Commission, Cashel Camp Site, Rowardenan, 0360-87234

Ferry:
A ferry runs from the Rowardenan Hotel to Inverbeg three times daily in the summer season. Some accommodation may be available at Inverbeg or you can connect with public transport.

Adjacent Hills:
Ben Lomond, 974 metres; start point, Rowardenan Car Park
OS 56, Grid Ref. 359986

Route:

The Way skirts the grounds of Rowardenan Youth Hostel and leads to a point where you are given a choice of either a single track along the lochside or a Land Rover track through the trees. The track through the trees offers an easier alternative but after several kilometres the two rejoin to become single track along the shore. The track weaves through the trees to reach Inversnaid, where you can stop at the hotel for a coffee and biscuits.

Inversnaid

Shops:
None.

Hotels:
Inversnaid Hotel, Inversnaid, 0877-86223 A

Hostels:
None.

B&B's:
None.

Campsites:
There is no camping generally allowed between Inversnaid and Inverarnan. Please contact the Inversnaid Hotel if you wish to camp. There is a small campsite a quarter of a mile to the north of the hotel.

Tourist Information:
Tourist Information, Aberfoyle to book, 08772-352

Adjacent Hills:
Stob an Fhaine, Beinn a Chroin 769 metres; start Inversnaid Hotel, OS 56, Grid Ref. 337089

Route:

This is probably the most arduous part of the whole West Highland Way. The going is solely on single track following the loch shore. Part of the track is boggy but otherwise very good. The path wanders in and out through the trees. The track passes Doune Bothy which is an example of the work done by the Mountain Bothies Association and is open to all as a shelter for the night. From here you quickly reach the end of Loch Lomond about four kilometres from Inverarnan. The RSPB nature reserve next to the Inversnaid Hotel is worth a detour and there are waymarked paths and a prepared leaflet of the reserve.

Inverarnan

Shops:
Ardlui 1 1/2 miles back down A82
(Access to Ardlui by Ferry, Summer Only)

Hotels:
Ardlui Hotel, Ardlui, 03014-243 B
Inverarnan House Hotel, Inverarnan, 03014-234 A

Hostels:
None.

B&B's:
Various; contact Tourist Information, Tarbert to book 03012-260

Campsites:
There is some camping allowed at Beinglas Farm, phone 03014-281/289 for permission.

Adjacent Hills:
Beinn Chabhair, 933 metres; start Beinglas Farm, OS 50/56, Grid Ref. 322187

Route:

The Way wanders round the back of Beinglas farm then along a sound Land Rover track for about a kilometre before it becomes single track. This is a well constructed part of the Way and the going is sound. There are some spectacular waterfalls on the River Falloch along this section. From Derry Darroch the track gets a little boggy in parts before crossing under the main A82. On the west side of the road, the track changes back to a Land Rover track and winds its way up to the top of the hill overlooking Crianlarich where a single track leads either to Crianlarich or to Tyndrum.

Crianlarich

Shops:
Grocer/Supermarket/News.

Hotels:
Ben More Hotel, Crianlarich, 08383-210 C
Alt-Chaorain House Hotel, Crianlarich, 08383-283 B
Craigbank Guest House, Crianlarich, 08383-279 A
Glenardran Guest House, Crianlarich, 08383-236 A

Hostels:
Crianlarich Youth Hostel, Crianlarich, 08383-260

B&B's:
Various; phone Tourist Office, Tyndrum to book, 08384-246

Camping:
There is no official campsite in this area. Please ask permission before camping.

Adjacent Hills:
Cruach Ardrain, 1046 metres, Ben Tulaichean, 946 metres;
Ben More, 1174 metres, Stob Binnien, 1165 metres;
Start point, Crianlarich for both pairs. OS 51, Grid Ref. 385254

Route:

Single track leads you out of Crianlarich and over the little hill above, to get good views over Strath Fillan. The Way continues on a single track over the Hervie Burn till Kirkton Farm, crossing the A82 on the way. Walking is on Land Rover track till you cross the road again and then on single track till you find your way into Tyndrum.

Mileage	Possible Mileage	Planned Mileage
Milngavie		
5		
Carbeth	Day One 12 Miles	
7		
Drymen		
6		
Balmaha	Day Two 14 Miles	
8		
Rowardenan		
7		
Inversnaid	Day Three 20 Miles	
7		
Inverarnan		

Fort William **Start/Finish**

Kinlochleven

Kingshouse

Bridge of Orchy

Tyndrum

Crianlarich

Inversnaid

Rowardenan

Balmaha

Drymen

Carbeth

Start/Finish **Milngavie**

Mileage	Possible Mileage	Planned Mileage
Inverarnan		
6		
Crainlarich		
6		
Tyndrum	Day Four 14 Miles	
8		
Bridge of Orchy		
12		
Kingshouse	Day Five 20 Miles	
8		
Kinlochleven		
15	Day Six 15 Miles	
Fort William		

Tyndrum

Shops:
Supermarket/News, Clifton Coffee House & Gift Shop
The Green Welly Shop, Outdoor Wear & Kit, Well worth a visit, even if only for a fresh pair of socks.

Banks:
There are retail banking facilities at the Clifton Coffee House/Green Welly Shop-Cost £1 per £50 cashed.

Hotels:
Invervey Hotel, Tyndrum, 08384-219 A
Royal Hotel, Tyndrum, 08384-272 A

Hostels:
Pine Trees Caravan Site, Bunkhouse, Tyndrum, 08384-243

B&B's:
Various; contact Tourist Information, Tyndrum to book, 08384-246

Camping:
Pine Trees Camp Site, Tyndrum, 08384-243
Camping is not normally allowed between Tyndrum and Bridge of Orchy.

Adjacent Hills:
Ben Challum, 1022 metres; start point Kirkton Farm, OS 50, Grid Ref. 356281;
Ben Dubhcraig, 978 metres, Ben Oss, 1029 metres; Ben Lui, 1130 metres; start point OS 50, Grid Ref. 344293

Route:

This is possibly one of the easier sections of the Way, climbing out of Tyndrum along Land Rover track for a short while, before dropping to level ground for the walk through to Bridge of Orchy. About 500 metres of this section is along single track. The rest is on Land Rover track right through to Bridge of Orchy Station.

Bridge of Orchy

Hotels:
The Bridge of Orchy Hotel, 08384-208 A
Inveroran Hotel, 08384-220 A

Bunk House:
The "Way In" Bunkhouse, Bridge of Orchy Hotel, 08384-208

B & B's:
None at Bridge of Orchy, although several within 3 to 4 miles of the Way.

Tourist Information:
Tourist Information Centre, Tyndrum, 08384-246

Camping:
There may be some camping please ask at either The Bridge of Orchy Hotel or The Inveroran Hotel

Adjacent Hills:
Beinn Dorain,1074 metres, Beinn an Dothaidh,1002 metres; start point Bridge of Orchy Station OS 50, Grid Ref. 300395
From Inveroran : Stob Ghabhar,1087 metres, Stob Choire Odhar, 947 metres; start point Victoria Bridge, OS 50, Grid Ref. 271422

Route:

A short climb over the hill takes you from Bridge of Orchy over to Inveroran and the climb is well worth the effort for the views. The next section of the Way, together with the following section over the Devil's Staircase, is possibly the most exposed and mountainous section of the Way, curving round the side of the mountains and running across the edge of Rannoch Moor. The going is very good along Land Rover track all the way through to Kingshouse and although exposed, swift progress can be made. The views over to the Bridge of Orchy Hills are super and on a clear day you can enjoy some lovely views over the Moor.

Kingshouse

Hotel:
The Kingshouse Hotel, 08556-259 A

Hostels:
The Kingshouse Hotel, 08556-259

B&B's:
None.

Camping:
The Kingshouse Hotel, 08556-259

Adjacent Hills:
Sron na Creise, 1068 metres, Meall a Bhuiridh, 1108 metres, start point; White Corries, OS 41, Grid Ref. 265524:
Buachaille Etive Mor, 1022 metres, start point Altnafeadh, OS 41, Grid Ref. 222563; plus of course the whole of Glencoe, OS 41.

Route:

The Way now climbs to its highest section so far, over the Devil's Staircase on a winding single track, to a height of around 550 metres and then down into Kinlochleven. The going is good along the old military road from the Kingshouse Hotel, continuing for a short 500 metre section alongside the A82 before cutting onto single track over into Kinlochleven. After about 4 kilometres the track meets up with a Land Rover track to end up at sea level again at Kinlochleven.

Kinlochleven

Shops:
News, Baker, Supermarket, Hardware.

Bank:
The Royal Bank of Scotland, Kinlochleven. Open Thursdays.

Post Office

Hotels:
The McDonald Hotel, Kinlochleven, 08554-539 B
Mamore Forest Lodge Hotel, Kinlochleven, 08554-213 B

Hostels:
West Highland Lodge Bunkhouse, Kinlochleven, 08554-471
Mamore Forest Lodge Hotel, Kinlochleven, 08554-213

B & B's:
Various; contact Tourist Information Centre, Fort William to book, 0397-703781

Camping:
McDonald Hotel, Kinlochleven, 08554-539

Adjacent Hills : The whole of the Mamores OS 41

Route:

The walk starts with a steep pull out of Kinlochleven to reach the old military road through the hills to Fort William. This is on single, well constructed track till you meet the road. The road passes for about 8 kilometres between the hills which can be quite exposed, before beginning to drop as you reach the shelter of the trees. After a short while, the Way becomes single track again as it wanders through the trees to link up with the forestry roads as you drop into Glen Nevis and Fort William.

Fort William

Shops:
Fort William has got the lot!

Banks:
Royal Bank of Scotland, Bank of Scotland, Clydesdale, TSB.

Post Office

Hotels and Accommodation:
Contact the Tourist Information Office which is open all year round to book your accommodation. Fort William has a wide variety of hotels, guest houses, bed & breakfast, youth hostels and bunk house accommodation.
Fort William Tourist Information Centre, 0397-703781

Travel:
British Rail, Fort William Travel Centre, 0397-703791
Skyeways, Kyle of Lochalsh, 0599-4328
GaelicBus, Ballachulish, 08552-229
Scottish Citylink Coaches, Glasgow, 041-332-9191

West Highland Way Diary

My Experiences on the West Highland Way

and Yours

West Highland Way Diary

Day 1

Will I ever make it, 95 miles? Set out from Milngavie Station and look for turn off in the town. Well marked and going easy through the town and into park. Soon clear houses and into countryside proper. Weather dry and set to remain so. Lunch at Dumgoyne. Next 2 miles appalling, mud with consistency of cement and glue. After joining road into Drymen it gets better. Hope this is the worst. Very quiet, have only met 6 people and 3 of them are out for the day. Cross field and cut back into Drymen for night. Next day seems promising and terrain looks interesting.

Day 2

Weather Glorious. Bright sunny day. If it stays like this for the next 5 days, things will be fine. Out of Drymen on the main road for 100 yards before pulling onto the verge, cutting across a field and into the woods. Very quiet walking. After walking for 1 1/2 miles meet first person, lady walking her dog in Garadhban Forest. Route over Conic Hill closed for lambing, closed for 4 weeks April/May. Walk down alternative route via Milton of Buchanan and along main road to Balmaha. Main road a bit of a drag. Climbed hill at Balmaha (Craigie Fort) for views along Loch Lomond. Weather too hazy for good photo but worth the effort. Track now weaves along loch and roadside. From Sallochy Way runs along lochside through the trees to Rowardenan. Beginning to feel yesterdays exertions, glad to see Youth Hostel. Much changed since schooldays, very comfortable. Up to 6 to a room, 3 in mine.

Day 3

What a change in the weather. Where has all the sun gone? Damp and wet this morning. Early start for long day planned. Alternative route along forest road, easier going. Track through trees to Inversnaid beginning to get more difficult. Coffee and biscuits at Inversnaid. RSPB nature trail at Inversnaid, wish I had time to stop. Track along lochside very tough since dodging through mud and tree roots. Stop at Doune Bothy for lunch & a brew. Two lads have decided that this is enough for today and gone off to look for firewood. From Ardleish, track begins to climb over shoulder of

West Highland Way Diary

Day 1

Day2

Day 3

Cnap Mhor and down towards Inverarnan. Into Glen Falloch for pull up to Crianlarich. Going easier at first but long day and feeling tired. Derry Darroch next target after here. Seems easier until walk under Railway, very low tunnel, legs almost give way. Uphill all the way to Crianlarich now, seems forever. Youth Hostel very modern, after hot shower, dinner and a pint of Guiness, much better.

Day 4

Short pull out of Crianlarich to top of previous day's hill. Views over Glen Dochart both East and West. Weather damp, may improve. Quick walk up to Tyndrum for coffee, scone and a piece of flapjack. Buy 4 Mars bars for lunch and emergencies! Steep track out of Tyndrum along old road before single track for a while, then back onto old road. Blisters on heel, first of walk and own fault for not tying boots tightly. Dressed from First Aid Kit and hope for best. No more trouble for rest of walk. Keep passing ladies from some walking club. At least I can still overtake ladies 30 years older than me, I can't be that bad. Easy going to Bridge of Orchy. Check route goes over hill to Inveroran. Is it better to go round by road? Wander wearily up to hill, super views of Bridge of Orchy hills and over Loch Tulla. Well worth the effort. Drop to Inveroran to check into hotel. 2 hours kip before dinner. Food great, even better that I don't do cooking.

Day 5

Massive breakfast, late start, not till 9.30. Easy track over to White Corries and Kingshouse but bit exposed. Views good but cloudy. Rain threatens. 12 noon rain starts and does not let up all day. Kingshouse for lunch. Bowl of soup a meal in itself!
Difficult to leave to go out into rain, sleet and wind again. Boggy to Altnafeadh but Devil's Staircase to come. Fly up Devil's Staircase. What's wrong? Sleet and wind over top, no stopping till Kinloch-leven. Rain and wind have not let up for hours. Bunkhouse up on hill. Was I spoilt by last nights hotel? Opening door reveals a thick cloud of smoke caused by 4 young lads playing cards and emptying cans of Tennants. The Youth Hostels have spoilt me for this. Go out for supper to try to dry off.

Day 4

Day5

Day 6

The Last Day. Wet and windy again. Why me? Steep track out of Kinlochleven to connect with Military Road through the Mamores. At least wind and rain at my back. Shelter in old barn at Tigh na Sleubhaich for a brew and 2nd breakfast. Reach trees as rain stops. Back on to single track for final climb into Glen Nevis. Track bobs and dips giving weary limbs trouble. Watch new born lamb try to find its lunch from mother who offers no help at all. Drop down forest road to reach Glen Nevis Road and 1 1/2 miles into Fort William and finish. Meet friend and scrounge lift home. A perfect end.

Day 6

Notes